Love Is a Burning Building

and other Birthday Poems
(with one farewell poem)

J. P. Dancing Bear

FUTURECYCLE PRESS
www.futurecycle.org

Cover art, "Stained Glass Abstract," by Kristen Slye Smith; cover and interior book design by Diane Kistner (dkistner@futurecycle.org); author photo by C. J. Sage; Chaparral Pro text with Libel Suit titling

Published by FutureCycle Press
Hayesville, North Carolina, USA

ISBN 978-1-938853-56-2

Contents

Acknowledgments

Lung

it's your birthday: and the lungs are at it again: they refuse to believe that they are not inward wings: and so when you daydream: they prepare for flight: they send signals to the brain: they tell it a dream of pink wings soaring over the white landscape of winter: and the weird thing is the brain provides a soundtrack to this fantasy: something like Miles: and with every note: the lungs are inhaling: or exhaling: as if they might be the great musician's: and as the lungs begin to pass: more landscape: they expand: they grow larger: and your body is now the size of bronchial tubes: the lungs are soaring higher and faster: you are not in control and the brain has strapped on a helmet and is lifting its hands in the air like this is a roller-coaster ride: oh what can you do: be thankful the lungs do not want: to remind you of every smoky jazz bar and gin joint you've ever visited: I guess: but hey: the music in the jazz joints was pretty good: almost worth it

for Don Stabler

Dust and Stars

you close your eyes and you can hear the stars: they are white birds: spiraling high above the field mice of our souls: or they are atomic and too small: for our imaginations to believe they are anything but large and distant: one photon feather chasing: its opposite: not-opposite: particle of a particle: you love how they have been everywhere in the universe: while you have stayed here hugging the planet: sometimes there are no words for this love you feel: like the great spaces between galaxies: everywhere and all at once: and if someone says *dark matter*: then so be it: a particle breaks out of its orbit: becomes something new and else: singing a different law into memory: you can hear beyond the musical veil of stars: the breaths of other people: living their own closed eyes: sloughing their particles: changing slowly into something else: you are smiling: listening to one atom bounce off another: was it one of yours: leaving or becoming you?: the body sloughs all its cells within seven years: that's what a scientific friend said: house dust is made of you: when you visit or are visited: part of us stays behind: is breathed in: becomes us: the folds in the veil feel like your own hair: string-theorying along between the little starbirds

for Maxine Hong Kingston

The Garden of Hours

the garden holds all your life: each timepiece is a moment that you wish to remember: one is the body of a lover you only remember by curves: there is fruit on the branches and the ghosts of gold leaves: this season-less place: this garden of metaphor and private symbology: you know what each crack in the wall means: what the water flowing reflects: that bare branch that bears its meaning to you only: you walk to the wellspring: the water is flowing fine here: a statue touches its heart: a clock sprouts wings: Spanish moss catches the wind and whistles a little: there's a strange desire to get busy: to do something: but you glance at one of the clock faces and sit down with your feet dangling into the water: it's as you suspect: you've got time

for David Nolan

At Night the City Rearranges Its Buildings to Speak to You

the city looks like a broken alphabet to you: a series of sentences that you can't read: and so there's a need: to make sentences: you write down the words: you call them *sketches of the city*: every time it is a different sentiment: sure, Dr. Jung would be laughing: because he wants to tell you the city's a reflection of self: but sometimes the city whispers things you did not know were true: you don't think it's so wrong: to have a little magic in your city: or to believe it holds messages only you can read

for Patrice Olivier

Grade School Guernica

it all starts when you tell Henry Miller that Ernest Hemingway's dad can kick his dad's ass: the next thing you see are the playground horrors of war: the carousel horses are the first tragedy: no match for the modern advances in model airplanes: the toy bombardiers: the doll eyes rolling away: balloons lose the grasp of hands and fly into the grave sky: a wooden arm holding a sword: set aflame by careless strikings of matchbooks: O the terrible dead plastic babies: and the little pigtailed girls crying for them: it's a free-for-all: Henry and Ernest: like bull's horns and striped carousel lances: O the scarred knees: the broken fingers: the skinned elbows: we carry forward onto greater playgrounds

for Paul A. Toth

Songbird

the paper does not try to be a metaphor of a bird: even though your inner songbird sees the avian outline: the breeze makes it waver and sway: sometimes expanding: which you interpret as puffing the chest: possible mating ritual: black ink smudging its story and headlines to gray: a wing of a famous face: blue water for a beak: here you sing of glorious figures: smooth feathers: and the thrum of hearts: you fly around to nearby bushes: bring back the small berries of love: an offering: but it makes no move at them: look sideways and up to the newsprint face: the wind blows strong enough to make folded paper fly: spread out from its crumpled bird form: into a single wing: looping and spiraling in flight: you sing a frail tune for the silhouette of a soaring: you look at the berries: a full meal: you've worked up such a hunger

for Nate Pritts

Fanning Out

your rays are golden feathers: fanning out third-eye star: quills piercing the reality of skin: your cheeks blush: to match the aura of red hair: a ruff of clouds around your collarbone: you say the word *pinnacle*: this day you walk out into the world: where others fan their hearts: other organs: other flesh: the boy with the blue quills rising out of his shoulder: foot haloed: a spleen's headdress: crowns of aches and pangs: ghosting in vanes: you wear an eagle's nest for a hat: face the dawn: breathe in light: take it deep into your lungs: earth – water – light: melding into the thrumming within your chest: you keep a steady gaze: ready to exhale wisdom: should anyone ask

for Diane Penrod

Icarus in Twilight

you blame the lucky one who gets off the island on first try: for telling
your story wrong: you are retold: the one who got too close to the sun:
the fallen: this much is true: there was always enough wing left to slow
yourself descent: not to completely crash: you swam back to shore: re-
sketched the diagrams: built better wings: hours of sewing canvas: the
rigging lines: the frames: to rise up close to the sun: and come down
again: and again: more schematics: more geometry and algebra: finer
thread: which you wove yourself: calculations for tensile strengths: and
now: soaring anywhere you wish to: you realize the unlucky one: broke
out on the first try: what you've learned about the fine detail and science
of flying and wings: takes you beyond a mere escape

for Andrew Demcak

Temple of the Ocean

you've walked along the beach for hours: taking in the energy of each wave offered: you fill yourself with blue and green light: wade into the water heart-deep: to feel the power sway you as it swells in and draws out: when it pulls: it is like a lover's needs: the water over the stones and sand singing to you: a wooing voice: each wave is an arm in a dance: timed perfectly to meet your body: on the shore there wait treasures: ornate shells: stones polished by the surf: sand dollars: a speckled feather: the rainbow interior of an abalone shell: you run your finger along the lip: of the swirling greens, blues, and purples: almost like the currents: the ocean catches the sun itself with its ropes of mists and fog: bright golden light: even as you step back onto dry sand your spirit says *yes, yes, yes*: and this is why you love the ocean back with everything within you: the primal call of each wave: the power: without ego: each graceful wave: willing to accept you as you are: willing to give you all that it can

for Lorna Dee Cervantes

Presto

somehow even the most impossible things find a way to kiss: abraca-
dabra: you are watching porcupines nuzzle on the animal station: which
you are sure is really the anthropomorphosis station: *pick a card– any
card*: kicking back in your sorcerer's chair: changing golden eggs to red
potatoes: to small gas giants: just for the irony: *a bouquet of scarves*: you
turn porcupine quills into lances: the sign reads: *jousting at 6pm: – wear
your best armored tuxedo*: and you quote: *by the pricking of my thumb…*:
and someone behind you in the long line sings a serenade to needles: you
change the channel: to "fashion week": *look mom– no hands*: it's a pretty
slick life: —making the broom do all your housework: doves and bunnies
romp and dive: outside your window: *and now for my next trick…*

for Anders Larsson

16

The Leaving Bees

you could see from here: the Frank Lloyd Wright of the bee architects: had been working hard: had created a new platform: and you wondered if this was evolution: already efficient by design: had they kicked it into overdrive: as if the threat to their species was an alarm: a siren: or maybe this is the bee haven: the retreat in the mountain woods: the bee citadel: have they escaped us: what if in their quantum language: they heard Einstein's words: but left instead of waiting to die

for Bienenstock Thee Zeitschrift

Soft Watch Put in the Appropriate Place to
Cause a Young Ephebe to Die and Be Resuscitated...

O Time: O ghosts: O soft watches: we think so much of our time: and our ghosts and hope: that our internal clocks will soften: like ripe brie: O third-eye clock dreaming: dreaming of the slow hands making their way: oblong and elliptical: through the space of mind: O young hero: out there on the rocks: painting them colorful and dramatic: O dynamic artist-atomic: you are there: with statues: brilliant white and tragically posed: begging for color: O pigmentor: what is time: if not the yellowed ghost of color: rising at sunset: tag this moment: with a polyethylene blue and cadmium red: stop it at the gates: keep it from escaping: this is always on your watch

for Visual Piracy (aka Neil Women158 Parkinson)

Cowgirl Guernica

you may have instigated the whole thing: you know: what with telling the cowgirls (half cow/half girl) to pay attention to the dwindling buffalo: it didn't take much: just one more loser cowpoke: staring at a nice set of udders is all: they never saw it coming (again—too busy staring at udders): the CGs overtook the covered wagon: and the stage: all headed west: they shot the sheriff: *AND* the deputy: and burned down the town with the sunset: left a pyre of mannequins: over-proportioned Barbie dolls of objectification: bags of money in the back of the coach like breasts: they could go to Hollywood: make a movie: live on the edge of the world: write a book: about rebellion: rewritten into a screenplay: to take place in the glorious Western mythos

for Barbara Shomaker

Sleep with Accordions and Divers

it's all oxygen hoses and rusted diving helmets in your sleep: you're curled up on the dock again: on a mattress of old maps of the sea floor: old hose attachments for vacuuming sand: away from relics: while dueling divers play *Sweet Gypsy Rose*: by accordion light: the glass of your helmet fogs: you can barely make out the other divers around: but you can hear a child giggling in her own suit: fuel drums uneasily next to the winch: everyone is waiting for the song to end: all the gear is packed: you readjust your pillow: like heavy equipment hitting the sea floor

for Lee Ann Brown

A Bed and Two Night Tables Attack Ferociously and Violently

all night the bed was fighting with the night tables: it was just like when you used to live in the apartment: underneath the family of fighters: there would be a loud crash: lots of yelling and slamming and crying back then: you hate it when your furniture fights: first you know how they tell you never to go to bed angry: well it's even more the case when the bed's angry: you don't want to sleep in an angry bed: and then there's the way the nightstands look at you: like they know you were the one who called the cops on them the other night: it's a terrible position the furniture pieces have put you in: having to tiptoe around them like that: and what about that time they beat up your cello: then claimed it was in self-defense: a defenseless cello! they're animals: no you were better off sleeping on the couch last night: the couch with its wide open loving arms: always there to take you back: always watching over you as you fall asleep

for James Maughn

Disintegration of the Persistence of Memory

the soft clocks are melting: while the universe breaks: down: to atomic sub-particles: the lip of the ocean is peeling back: old paper curling: layer after wave: fish know not where to school: even after timepieces convert: to a liquid state: small pools for fish to eye: enviously: when everything recedes to building-block basics: do the engineers go too: do you view the synapse: half empty or full: all those cells merging with the desire to become something new: you worry about what's happening: the consequence without acknowledging: the threshold: of each moment

for Cameron Baron Murray

Chrysalis

crack your statuesque chrysalis: the one that has reminded too many people: of a greek goddess: you leave it in the town square: with the water-stained fountain: that needs it: more than you do: walk down the street anew: fresh from your past self: walk differently: shoulders back: a proud stride: you see the curtains of the windows part: a finger and a nose: all the gawkers: recessed in their triangles of darkness: a frown of envy: you cannot worry about the faces of shadows: you are marching out to the tune of your new life: with any luck: what you've left behind is more than just the history: and tomorrow: there will be more statues in the plaza square

for Sheila Lanham

The Concert Audience

you listen for a moment in the small shrine of cats: a back alley in town: one musician crashes the symbols like garbage can lids: almost ready as the tuba player begins his homage to distant barking dogs: (necessary evil in the tale of cats): you begin the violin: one feline call: long and slow: and the orchestra follows: the first cat arrives: and sits: a perfect statue: near your side: listening to glorious night melody: soon others come: each closing their eyes: sitting upright: like Egyptian gods: suddenly unearthed and honored again

for Kari Tieger

Writing

today you sit down to write in longhand: you dress the part: in garb from another century: quill pen and inkwell: but this is only for mood and ambiance: you work through the process slowly: building stanzas: intricate metrics and geometry: tiered lines: words with angles: each as valid as the other: spheres orbiting refrains: edges are created: sections are not x'd out: so much as departed to begin new ideas: you embody the poem: taking on its features and angles: or it becomes a mirror: bringing to light those curves and corners you had not realized are there

for David Yezzi

Cypress

you spend all day climbing the mountain: sweat and dust: you see the
red-tail come in close and then bank behind a cloud: at the peak you see
the cypress: already taller than your last visit: it is like a swirling green
imitation of a cumulus cloud against the bright blue: high grass: slivered
white ghost of a moon: and the afternoon clouds already building:
coming in: you stay long enough for them to reach you: until you can
barely see the cypress and the edge: it is like being in a ghost world: as
though this is the place you stay when it's time: you hear the voices
telling you to go: while the daylight's good: one look back at the cypress
first: – *old friend, old friend*

for Pam Uschuk

Adam and Eve in the Garden of Guernica

first off: Eve is too smart for the caveman Adam: God is always pointing a finger at Adam's head: like there is something that still needs a divine reminder: Adam thinks God wants him to touch that cursor: it's all chickens and dinosaur eggs anyway: and which came first: a cell splits: a yoke divides like yin and yang: the super soldier goes all Incredible Hulk: or Buddha: or Dr. Moreau: the rotund Ronald clown is first in line at the Korova Milk Bar: God's still too busy deciding which country's side he's on: those demanding a blessing: or those who already think it's happened: the new metrosexual Adam finds a pillow: he wants brainy Eve to share it with him: the mythic love of his life: but she's a cross-the-t's-and-dot-the-petri-dish kind of woman: so off she goes to search the geologic record: looking for the missing link in his evolution

for Rebecca Skloot

Aimless Day

you say *today, I'm aimless*: as though you will be smashing compasses shortly: but it's not like that: the steady hands of the clocks gesture their circles: and you feel like walking: through the crowded streets: you overhear conversations: you can't keep them straight: one's story is all their stories: an old man playing chess: in the park: looks at you with the saddest eyes: he hands you a yellow rose: cupping your hands around it: nodding and laughing: the other old chessmen say you're pretty: and you spend the rest of the day smelling the rose: and wandering: and when you get back you pencil into your calendar: other days to be aimless

for Leslie Harrison

Flight and String

you say *marionette me*: and the birds you never thought were in this field: rise up: white doves: and strings: tying your arms: your body: your legs: *marionette me*: flocks of wings: fluttering around you: lifting you slowly at first: one arm at a time: *marionette me*: then a leg off the ground: your head rising: *marionette me*: you can feel feathers sprouting out of your body: as though this is what evolution is: the strings go taught: *marionette me*: and you can feel yourself move: walk: the strings of your jaw pull and release: and you are nearly speaking: nearly forgetting: your wish: *marionette me*

for Alexander Cigale

Chambers of In and Out

skylight of whale tails: and a fish on the line: old equations and formulas are carved into the walls: knight takes clock: but in his anthracite armor dreams of becoming dice: compass points and small pluses: it's all dove wings and jesus lizards with you: the superball you threw years ago: is still bouncing: even as the clouds slip through: you once studied the great pyramids: to reveal the pharaohs were overcompensating: —the monster trucks of their time: floor full of sky: you will not profess your love old crumbling plaster of Paris: though you stare at it for hours: each patch an outline: a silhouette of your next animus: you keep it all under henna tattoos: and though the heart has its four chambers: of stop and go: this one is your secret favorite

for Jennifer Sarah Cooper

Dog in the World

you say *there is something about a dog: that reflects the rest of the world*: in its perked up ears: wagging tail: ready for the next moment's joy: certain it will come: and the dog reflects the eagerness of the dog: off every appendage: as though its coat is one of mirrors: a million moments of happiness all within one moment: as the tail reflects the image of the ears: reflecting the body and the tail again: until the whole of the dog is shimmying: with excitement: and you cannot help but smile: which is reflected back at you: from so many different parts: and angles: of the dog

for Jessie Lendennie

Beyond Confusalem, USA

you're out for your morning roll: down the sidewalk in your radio-hat: talking on one cellphone and texting on the other: you've got your speaker knee pads on: your internet connections flapping in your wind: past the Confusalem storefront with its paper-hat barker-girl: *see the all new line of Gotopoxy toasters: it's a Red Dot Deal– today only*: past the Ouroboros fireplug dogs: it's already a bustle-as-usual day: on the main street: you speed by the TV guy: fiddling his own knobs: and the meter-head taxi driver: honking his way to fareness: you jump the Halloween plastic pylons: out into the clouded streets: billboards all turn their backs to you: even the megaphone man with the faux lizard boots: ducks inside: they know you don't feel them anyway: all that old school marketing jazz: makes you pick up speed: you gotta roll: keep moving: —a whirlwind arrow: on your compass-dial heart

for Aleah Sato

Oracle

for you it begins in the last vestiges of daylight: in your crimson dress: while others are bowing and saying their vespers: the ground cracks: for you: in your vision hot magma is just below: those fissures glowing bright orange: each splintering fracture: a tea leaf to read: symbols only your soothy eye can interpret: gas bubbling through lava: escaping: hisses its song of possible futures: each rock an animal soul: adds purpose and movement to the omens: above you: the clouds are roiling into more shapes: it is a satellite striking: the tuning fork of your bones: you move your limbs: you sway: in this twilight hour: where all edges converge: you try to tell anyone: who will listen

for Sydney Wade

We Might All Be Mayan Calendars

you wake up and see the world in round calendars: like Mayan: each person a special counting system: of days and years: you interlock with others: working together redefining time: some have strange seasons: some have monkeys, iguanas, and alligators for constellations: some have five-day periods of mourning for the dead: a few calculate the long count of days: green thumb calendars: almanac predictors: each turns to connect and reveal a previously hidden day: you discover the day of the tortoise sun: you smile: today's your lucky day

for Tracy K. Smith

How New Careers Are Started...

three balls hovering over the calm of the Pacific: and you wonder what happened to the juggler: was this his last trick: the tools of his trade left magically in the air: or is there a mishandled chain saw somewhere on the ocean floor: circled by sharks: did L.A. finally get to him: he walked back from the pier at the edge of the Golden West: gone back to Peoria: did he juggle knives in front of the wrong gang: you watch the balls: thinking tragedy—no comedy: only three balls—*beginner*: and with that magic word spoken: the balls come to you: rising to the curve of your palms

for Tony Barnstone

Margin of Silence

you talk about the *margin of silence*: this twilight hour: how it puts holes in the body: where the lungs and the diaphragm live: you say *this is the real Witching Hour*: voiceless: wrapped blind in a shroud: with the light boring through you: no—this is how you feel: as though you have taken a vow: and this moment when the sun is already past the shoulder of the earth: when night is rushing: this margin: when the animal shifts are beginning and ending: here where departure and entry are done in soundless respect: you sit taking in the quietude: the music of pause: here it would be so easy to plummet into prayer: sheet flapping in the wind: you say *in this hour I was a mere ghost: I did not wander outside my shell: I sat in the margin of silence: refusing to follow: refusing to leave*

for Moira Egan

Garden of Earthy Delights

recently you are noticing the tomatoes are running through the garden: teasing the cucumbers to chase: to come play in the turned earth: the flowers: the flowers: intoxication perfume: calling bees to their business: all the vegetables are acting strange: and you are standing most of the time: right in the middle: with your hands in your pockets: back pressed to the leaves: a little dazed: as though none of this is real: the pear is not dancing lewdly for the avocado: you were not just approached by a persimmon: the cabbage is not kissing the sunflower: it's like that old joke about something being in the water: you're sure: you should go lie down: take a nap (if you aren't already doing so!): call it a day: wake up tomorrow: pray for a normal garden

for Dinty W. Moore

Dog

first off: Dog knows you are watching: as you should be: even when you are trying to hide your observance of Dog: because Dog is the center of everything: is the universe: the world: the fountain in the desert of your life: an unending isle of wet-tongued delights: he is the one true Dog: all others are false dogs: not worthy of your attention: Dog is watching: you and over you: when you confide in him: he cocks his head at you: Dog says *enough about you: scratch behind my ears*: it is always very humbling to be in the presence of Dog

for Jack Large

Self-Portrait (not mine)

you are the man in the window: the watcher: although in certain light
you see your own reflection on the glass: you superimposed on your
picture of the city: a park in your eye: a highway for a jaw-line: in some
ways this is how you've always seen yourself: a thriving urban center:
ideas coming in and out: exchanges: some components concerned with
time: and today you feel you hold the key to the city: you are the
honorary mayor: and on this side of the glass: all you survey is yours
to command

for Larry Jaffe

The Procrastination Box

someone has left a shroud behind: near the open window: as if to say *now I go flying*: left on a stack of boxes: the sky is full of moisture today: yet nothing will cry: in the empty room you build strange geometry out of scraps of pipe and wood: ribbons tied to the shape of triangles: as though this might be a note of some kind: *read this for all the answers*: right after you spend scholarly years deciphering the language: you may roll your eyes now: who has the time for such things: the window is a mouth that glares hungrily: afternoon light coming in to frame an opposing wall: it is so quiet here: and the light demands your touch: you leave your robe on a box: you feel the bones of your arms hollow: skin sprouting feathers: you take a running start: to touch the light: which shimmers off of your new embodiment

for Karla Rogers

Pacific Horizon

we'd seen your boat upon the beach: and all day we'd been searching under sun: for some of us: we were looking forward to a chance to meet with you: others who shared their memories: wanted to talk to you again: some of us quoted your lines under the scant shade of palms: there was thirst upon our lips: yet we went on with our vigil: your lines were like cirrus clouds: they stayed in the sky for a long time: we gathered flowers to put in your boat: just so you'd know we were thinking of you: in case we missed you: but when we returned: only the impression in the sand was left of your craft: someone spotted it on the evening horizon: we could see it touching the sun: and I wondered as the sun took you with it: if anyone can be the same after that

for Craig Arnold

The Countess

no sooner than you don the dress: do the rose petals begin to break away from your hair: for clouds and ship sails: the milk maiden winds: cheeks puffed out: fill them: all the goblins leave their markets: vow to pursue the ribbons of your hair: rivers: eddy and swirl: your keepsake locket blows his horn of roses: more petals: more sails: much to the ire of Neptune and his daughters: serpents in the fists of sea: your coat adorned with the finest pearlescent shells: you are the countess moon: gravity pulling the heart of a sea god: more petals spiraling into the ocean: you've launched a thousand ships before sunrise: dropped as many poems into the bottles: bobbing on the surface: catching currents: each a love poem: to whomever finds your words

for Annie Finch

Hinged

you feel like a door: only holding your hinges: as though somewhere a
naked frame: is sobbing: in this light you like to think about the bright-
ness of the moon: someone holds a guitar neck like a goose: and sings
Istanbul– not Constantinople: and you have to laugh: other times you feel
like a giant tooth: rough-surfaced like the moon: but usually late at night:
before dreams of floss: someone holds a toothbrush like a rifle: and sings
hi-ho it's off to work we go: perhaps there is too much vodka in the world:
you are listening to a cricket calling out: among the starlight: like a
squeaky hinge: you sing the oil can serenade: swaying back and forth:
until the words work their way in with the pin

for Sam Witt

Waltz on Black Velvet

the whole night feels like it's been painted on black velvet: you keep your coyote close: you dress in a white gown that makes you think of ghosts: it's the flow of the thing: but you go with it: because part of it scares you: and you pull the red scarf to put the whole ensemble over the top: now you look ready for haunting: which again scares you: but you embrace fear: you put on a waltz: pull the frightening side of you closer: and dance: *1-2-3, 1-2-3*: now you let the coyote off the leash: it goes to the darkest corner and howls: and you laugh, you laugh: right into the grinning face of fear

for Larissa Shmailo

I Give You Fresno

this seems like the oddest gift to give: an entire city: and Fresno, no less, perhaps in the hopes that someone might actually utter the words: *we'll always have Fresno:* it's a giant grid city where most of the major street names are ordered as efficiently as algebra: but you would probably appreciate that kind of logical city planner while running late to an event: having left your directions on the dresser: other cities rely on their blemishes (aka landmarks) to navigate and give directions by: but you only need to know: what number street or the alphabet: to make it in Fresno proper: and yes: I know I've said that chaos and randomness can be gifts too: that the mole and the freckle are what make life interesting: but so is the mapping hand that thinks of you alone in a city: somewhere between the wrinkles of a tectonic plate: uneasily entering the city limits at twilight

for Jeff Johnston

Tongue Tied

such patterns on the tongue: your shirt the color of a wounded sky: you
are thinking of matching your language to the day: paisley and green:
spruce and bhutan pine: you calculate the weather: late March and
already you can only think in blooms: meteorologist says *marigold* and
first honeybee: you look outside and speculate on the toile sky: *it's not
the fashion* you say: you like to make a good impression: something
memorable like chalk diamonds on Paris rain: of course you know there's
a good chance you'll drip hummingbird on your tie before noon

for Daniel Bowman Jr.

The Image of Hunger in the Image of a Fish

you don't even see the fish at first: only the forks: almost marching: laying out the silhouette of the fins and tail: how many a body can feed: how each metal hand is reflected in the wet sand: a slicker side: some of them so shiny as to reflect the sky: others giving way to rust: the salt song of the sea: this corrosion: blood of the fish: not-fish: the yin-yang: what pangs lay in the negative space of the prongs: the song in the surf: wave after wave: rushing through the body: not-body: the sun is a lemon slice: flavoring everything: yellow and tart: it makes your lips pucker: thinking of the tang of it: so much so you see the body's scales and fins again: until: there is only the hunger of the fish: and the hunger for the fish

for Justin Courter

"The past is never dead. It's not even past."

—William Faulkner

one wave crashes on the shore and is quickly replaced with another: you think you remember every detail of it: the curl and white water: light shining through the body of the wave: the seaweed trapped inside: its sound roaring against sand: and then another perfect past comes in behind it: green light: foam: crest: spindrift: and though you know they are different: they begin to become the same wave: gorgeously hitting the shore: each new wave: unique in the singular moment of time: packaged as a trip you once took to the beach: which you continue to take again and again

for Erica Bernheim

Love Is a Burning Building

you say *love is a burning building*: then run in: to save the woman on the second floor: the one you've watched as she stood in the window: as you walked past her apartment: on the other side of the street: she always seems to be wearing red: whenever you go by: always in the window: as though she knew you were coming: and yes: you do have a tendency to be punctual: like a self-fulfilling prophecy: both of you doing something almost ritual: and now this fire: this urgency: you run through the flames: wrapped in a sheet: through trapped billowing smoke: you bound the stairs: you know the door: you kick it in: you pull her body into your arms: carry her out into the street: as you've always known you would: when you first struck the match: so many weeks before

for Francois K. Needles

The Sun in Its Jewel Case

the water is so still here: the close dark depths: giving way to the reflection of sky: further out: until it is hard to imagine a horizon: the sun is a pocket watch: half buried in cloud: resting in this jewel case of water: you cast your line: the only noise to break the silence: except one dragonfly: in and out among the reeds and stumps: old trees: whose stories have been swept away: to some lumber mill of currents and termites: you stare out to where your line finally touches water: watching it: more than feeling the line with your finger: that dragonfly keeps hovering around you: as though expecting you to yield a hidden bounty of mosquitoes: it lands on the rotted stump nearby: testing the air with its wings: you

for Derick Burleson

Harvest Concert

it's all fishhead and egghead music: they sit down and play their lemon guitars and onion mandolins: strings and frets going to grapevines and runner strings: the fruit: born in the wind as the leaves turn: as the sugar fills: she in her crust of bread ruffs: she becoming clouds: shading the horizon: harbinger girl of the season: he with his laces of last season's flowers: his lily pad pants: sings about a red and gold leaf boat flotilla: a fleet of subtle changes in the color and tone of the day: those colder nights: and turning a corner into snow: you're out there in the gusts: gathering the falling fruits: for darker months ahead: while these players keep strumming faster: keeping track of the passing time

for Bob Geldof

Birdhouse

there is a lighthouse at the top of Pablo Neruda's head: beautifully dangerous: warning the mermaids and sailors of each other: there is a cave of an ear: where a word is spoken and repeated: spoken and repeated: throughout time: a humming bird lives within his head: one eye a window: so many people peering in through the open curtains: the other trained on a book: acquiring a lexicon: like a hummingbird: there are tiny Nerudas fluttering in other people's heads: winding up words: cranking the music box of their souls: then his soul: the songbird cage: rattling with each turn: Nerudabirds' sonorous Spanish song: you hear the words untranslated: and nod

for William O'Daly

Autumnal

you climb the limbs: like you remember doing so many years earlier: the tree having maintained its size: while everything else from childhood has become smaller: you find familiar patterns in the bark: from up here: you can see more than you remember: the fields cut into their divided geometries: roads that lead from nowhere to nothing: the distant crackle and hum: of telephone poles: —electric cicadas in the wind: you watch the red-tailed hawk: a dot circling this tree: within you the spirit of a mouse is scurrying to cover: these days are your favorites: warmed by the October sun: watching the slow shadow of autumn overtake the land-scape: edge closer to this tree

for Frederick Barthelme

Not Persephone

tonight you're feeling a little vulturish: in your tuxedo: it's not a pomegranate on your silver tray: and she's not Persephone: but you offer it to her anyway: she is weary of the way the paring knife slides out of the wall: or how peeling paintings of your ancestors: framed as they are: revert to feathers: the curtains cascade to a pool: ripple and sway: a staircase next to them: that has no beginning: play Miles Davis: cool and sublime: dancing her closer to a painting of steps: spiraling up and away: you ask if it's okay: to call her by a mythical name: she hunches her shoulders: stares at the currents below: she's got that look in her eye: the one that says *I could make this work*

for Seth Abramson

Indoor Topiary and Forgiveness

you've so little use for chairs these days: that your living room is a topiary: bushes shaped like pears: oranges: melons: a fishbowl for a pond: a green lawn for carpet: persimmon tree: dropping its harvest on the grass: on one wall you've painted a doorway to eternal spring: small canal heading away toward the false horizon: you've chosen for the sky-blue walls: the portraits of people in shock or mild bewilderment: like the faces of your guests: lizards sun themselves within an opened end-table drawer: a butterfly arises from a broadleaf plant: catches the attention of a leaping fish: a wave of water spilling forward with the full weight of hunger: like all contained gardens: there is always something on the verge of going wrong: you palm the fish back into the righted bowl: replace the liquid atmosphere of its world: a more forgiving gardener: you do not exile the fish: nor blame the butterfly: or the flat-smiling over-observant lizards

for Bernard Rea

Nocturne

those city lights scraping along the bottoms of cumulus: the slow erosion of clouds: while the driving moon presses on: out here beyond the lake: you can feel grass pulling at your soul: with soft whispers: its love for field mice: darting through its scalp: even in this cold: where the reflection of the night's only pearl sits like ice upon the water: you can hear the whip-poor-will: calling out into the chill: a red light blinks in the city: with each cry of the bird: your eyes rise: above the lake: the tallest buildings: daggering through the clouds: fading into the canvas of night: stars caught in the weave: twinkling brightly through the thin gloom: you focus on one star: you imitate the call of a small bird: close to the ground: waiting for the corresponding blink in the skyline

for Patricia Fargnoli

The Harvest

you go out to the countryside to pick doughnuts with your dad: Robby
the Robot: it's the final days of harvesting: the reddening grass: the gold
and orange trees: plenty of glazed and sprinkles: crullers and maple-iced:
and not once does he utter the word *danger*: a milestone you think:
within your own dome: arms extending to pick the ripe soft circles from
the branches: they look like the rings of your own wrists: the holes of the
fried dough make them easy to pick without bruising: on the walk home:
your father explains *the nuts and the bolts*: awkward—and you keep from
sniggering: the small body of your soul: itching in its armored shell: your
father watching the cumulus on the horizon: barometer halo spinning

for Quincy R. Lehr

Seasonal Change

everything changes: but not fast enough to notice: the umbrellas and volleyball nets have been dwindling for weeks: now one or two will stand defiantly for a short while longer: it's not the weather that sends them away: it's not the dampness in your heart: that cloud you've been secretly carrying with you all these months: either: you might begin with counting grains of sand: you might think long and often about the sun-bleached wood fence: which keeps nothing out: nothing in: but is merely there for someone else's show: the shadows of the reeds lengthen: crisscross with the rippled marks of wind: the surf pounds out the beat: familiar and rhythmic: as though you were born with it: it continues to draw you here: long after the tourists have trunked their blankets and coolers: and driven off: you don't want to think about disturbing this world with your footprints: so you do not look back: gusts pouring off the sea: will erase them soon enough: you can walk for miles here: walk alone: the surf and breeze conspiring: so that you never find evidence of having been here before: sometimes you want to be this *new* in the world

for Lana Hechtman Ayers

Captain of Autumn

she calls you *the Captain of Autumn*: handing you the splitting pomegranate: like a crown jewel: already you can feel your birch bones turning bare: acorn buttons on your coat: you hold a red leaf over your harvest moon heart: the unraveling: the threadbare corn silk of your hat: that golden sway of wheat upon your face: making the expression of allegiance: of honor: she gives you the berries she wears in her hair: the seeds the seeds: to hold dormant in your hands: while the puffs of cottony clouds are beginning to follow you: an entourage for the fields: you are the ghosts of harvesters and harvest: the tiller in the aftermath: the harbinger of change

for Chuck Durfee

Man with Dog

Most of the time the man is a shadow in the dog's life: even now: trundling the sidewalks: the man is a minor tension on the leash: dog has to make the most of these times: there is the business of dogliness: a world (no matter how concrete) to smell: stop for other like-minds: it's all wags and chuffs this close to the ground: the man follows at the dog's leisure: scent of discards: all things making ways to the sewers: dog listens to the music coming up from the grate like some ophic dog rising up from love

for Jonathan Kevin Rice

Harvest of Arrows

because autumn is a series of harvests: arranged around the cyclical circle of a year: one moment you are flushed with summer heat: then you are swept up by the harvest songs: today: the arrows have come in: ripe on the neon signs: advertisements and streets: little omens of herding: go here: be there: turn left: you pull down an arrow: almost the size of yourself: that hung curving to a shop: lights within: their tungsten still tingling: you catch your limit: arrows that say *parking in the rear: all cards accepted here*: and you strap them to your car: hood and roof: one in the backseat: necessary: *they* say: for culling: keeping the arrows from over-populating: we're all doing our part: making sure they won't ruin the ecosystem: or starve themselves: next year

for Mackenzie Carignan

Stable-Library of the Clone Shepherd

shepherd: you come forward: in speckled-egg light: you first think of old snowdrifts: of larvae to some atomic-aged insect: you believe you can just call her on the fleece-lined phone: the flock have already told you they are not your furniture: *it's always about ewe, isn't it:* but all eyes are watching from anxious corners: would you disturb her counting: just to hear her voice talking to you: are they safe here in the library? you heard the wolves last night: little book-burners dancing around their bonfire: the songbook falls open to "Hello Dolly": you can't see it: but instinct says she's got muck boots on: she's watching the flock too: but they think they've been watching over her: lock the door: lower the light: huddle: everyone will watch over every one tonight

for Lindsay Wilson

Flagmen in Autumn

they arrive with the first winds of the season: flagmen to slow us down: the work unseen: wait in your car: slow crawling: as the newspapers tumbleweed roll and spin across the road: plastic pylons knocked over with sudden gusts: the sky: ever darkening: marbles these men with shadow: their flaming vests: strange authority: page nineteen of yesterday's sunnier news flying: past the windshield: a bizarre bird: fearfully escaping the oncoming storm: all the cars at this intersection are colors of autumn: the traffic signs are leaves: ready to turn: ready to slip away with the next gust

for David Weinglas

The Spirit in Flight

there by the side of the road: you can see the spirit ready itself for flight:
even as the sheet of night unfurls: Mercury burning white: hot over the
place: where the sun fell: the soul stops to pose: something dignified:
purposeful: red heart on its sleeve: like an offering: one traveler to
another: you hear the old voices of the past: *it's not the destination...*
you love the blueness of the twilight: like a chord in that concerto: that
when played: will always bring a tear to your eye: you stop where the
ghost had been: ready to set up camp for the night: striking a dignified
stance: waving to the spirit: now fast on its way

for Ron Mohring

The Rites of Autumn

you've been building a nest in your head: from the twigs and branches: the undergrowth of your body: you say all the ritual words: forgivenesses and prayers: but like they were leaving your mouth for the first time: born into the chilling air: there is no restraining of feelings: you pull back the vines of your chest: and reveal the den within: sighing with the open space: each year you light the necessary fire: beginning the burning and regrowth: the splitting open of seeds: the rooting: into the earth: now the bird of your spirit returns: refreshed and ready for the new year

for Red Hand

DeBirdcage

you say *ponder why the caged birds sing later*: you swing the door open:
red bodies escaping: a few feathers spiraling: sticking into the grass:
grabbing the bars: you think you are going to tear it apart with your
hands: but there is no give in the construction: you throw it to the
ground: door rattling off: you kick it up into the air: more bars snapping
free as it lands: you stomp on the cage: which smashes flat: you are
looking for the jailer: a little man with a key—no one: you bend to pick
up one of the crimson tongues in the blades: you see the newly freed:
hopping from branch to branch: one following quickly behind the other:
still full of song: now full of joy

for Sandra Simonds

Otherology

one does not look directly at: while one will stare straight into: the photographic eye: one can spot distance: recited in numbers: while one gets a sense of what is in the frame: and not: one is meticulous as a stop watch: counting out the distance of thunder from lightning: while one is capturing the mood of light: the multifaceted clouds: one is measuring the space between breaths in the sweetgrass: while one is certain of prairie ghosts living in the tall grass: one is going back over the equations: while one is saying a prayer to the setting sun: one will not refer to his friend as something he is not: while one believes his companion is missing a shot

for Gerry LaFemina

Like Being Stuck in the Middle of Tennessee

you says it's all like being stuck in the middle of Tennessee: with
Arkansas roadmaps: with the radio dial stuck on Alabama: with expired
Kentucky license plates and an urge to drive: itchy for western North
Carolina: someone in the backseat is humming a Grand Ole Opry tune:
can you believe it: didn't you already turn off the radio: now this: it's
enough to make you break out the British Invasion: it's enough to make
you count sheep: dress up in a gawky ball gown: wait for rain: go on and
make a call: nudge someone's answering machine

for Angelia Stinnett

Eating Cezanne

you hunger-sneak: enter into the room and smell peaches: they sit here so close to the edge: what if you bumped the table with your hip: they'd all bruise-bounce and roll: maybe worse: torn flesh and bleeding juice: a sticky place you'll remember every time you walk by: sugar song: come closer with your utensil: *don't you know it's impolite not to offer*: they are almost too ripe: the color beginning to turn: it's a shame to let them fall prey to neglect: crazy damn painters: no wonder they starve all the time: they're too busy capturing the light reflected from food: the ominous shadow of fruit: go ahead and bite one: hunger is more easily understood than art

for Richard Peabody

Minotaur

outside the walls of this elaborate cage are street sounds: people in various states of betrayal: while the artist remains blocked in: shifting walls: Icarus saw the iris of it before falling: the watchful pupil dilated and fixed: roundhouse: the Jesus bull in the pit of the eye: he takes everything the world sends over the edge and turns it to paint: he says the word *love* at the foot of the spiral stairwell: and he hears it echo through the underworld: he starts with crimson: surreal turnstile house: each wall a canvas he paints with love

for Paul Guest

Mr. Parrotfish

you are pretty sure no one has seen you come to the surface: your parrotbeak cap firmly on: exhaling more clouds into existence: they rise like calves joining the darkening herd above: you sense the lightning in the distance: yet here the water is calm: you cock your head: listening, listening: for the siren song of parrots: you hear through the approaching storm: you listen past thunder and crashing waves: you pick them up somewhere in the South: hundreds of miles away: babbling on about a jungle fruit: tasty nuts: the lack of humans: you squawk and whistle excitement: then take in a deep breath: your face lit by a flash of lightning: back under the surface you go: racing the porpoises: dreaming the crack of brazil nuts: the rich oil of macadamias

for Daniel Kaczmarek

The Little Bird of Self

everyone says that the little birds tell them things: always spying: always keeping tabs on your friends: but you know this feathered pal too well: he's no tattling rat with wings: how his message gets turned around: is a problem of interpreters: he has always spoken about the freedom to fly: to be whatever you wish: to make the first leap: into wilderness: in this dawn light: firing the horizon: like hope itself: the bird circles you: around your feet and shoulders: like a chant: he repeats: and repeats: what the little friend tells you: holds true: the hardest part of flight: is believing in your wings

for Bob Cumming

Indefinite Divisibility

you can almost get a handle on this: monstrosity that you've been building: sometimes it's a machine that duplicates other things: other times it is the shadow of an insect: you collected shells: filled them like bowls: with salt water: now you cannot tell: which bowls were copied from originals: you pull a lever and hold on: as it bounces and pogos: you've fallen in love with the shadow of your creation: just like so many other creators: you lovingly: dutifully adjust the footing: it sounds like the ocean is laughing at you: or maybe it's the bowls of duplicated water: or the praying mantis appendage: of your machine: *it's okay* you say: the greatest work attracts the greatest critics

for Luigi Monteferrante

Morning Light and a Late Snow

you say *this is what I think I like about you*: and then there is a silence like
sunlight through white stained glass: she smiles: not Mona Lisa-like: not
Kate Moss-like: you are twisting the sheets: each time you roll over: and
all you can see through the window are animals breathing: as they are
herded away to Smokestack City: still she says nothing: like snow on the
North Pole: naked she walks to the framed panes: ripples in each inlay of
glass: edges frosted: she is a curve: she is a turnpike: a highway: washed
in snowlight: and you are a small fox padding the banks through flurries:
daring to cross to the other side

for Gordon Massman

Through Winter

you are riding through snow again: thinking this should change to reflect the weather of the waking world: the antler trees sing their songs of rebirth: already they desire the tiny buds of green: they feel the earth warming under white curtains: it's time for the other half of the world to cool off: blue music where once was gray: you want a new picture of yourself: something green: you think you could be Persephone: with flowers in your hair: the trees greenly agree

for Diane Kirsten Martin

Anura

you say the word and a frog arcs into the air: it doesn't matter where you are: say it enough times really fast: you get a biblical response: this is your gift: your superpower: which may not seem like much: to be the amphibian queen: how many nights did you stay awake thinking of your alter ego's name: *Anura*—intelligent without all the baggage: you once stopped a group of debs from picking on a nerd: with a leaping green body for each mean girl: you stopped a bank robbery with a rain of frogs: stunned: mouths agape: they froze there watching the sky: dumb really: when you think about it: guessing it was God's immediate inter-vention for their sins: and the cops took them away: —crime in the area was down for a whole year after that: the credit never went to you: *divine intervention* stole the headlines again: but you were never in this for the attention

for Stephanie Kartalopoulos

Your Robot Girl

you theorize you have enough parts to build the robot: discarded mannequins: doll parts: discarded hydraulic pumps: servos and gears: gyroscopes and motors: you dream of a positronic brain: but you can't wait for someone to believe in it: sidewalk ants may have to do: the hive mind: enough workers to move the parts and push the buttons: you train them: the simplest eye-blink and a finger twitches to begin: she watches that butterfly: the hunger of the masses behind each eye: you will not waste her talents on domestic monotony: you teach her to harness her hunger into writing: hoping only that she will acknowledge you: as a character in one of her novels

for Michelle Grimes Shamasneh

Acknowledgments

An Autumn Anthology: "Autumnal," "Captain of Autumn," "The Harvest," "Harvest Concert"

Ante Room: "A Bed and Two Night Tables Attack Ferociously and Violently"

Assisi: An Online Journal of Arts & Letters: "The Image of Hunger in the Image of a Fish"

Blip: "Anura," "Soft Watch Put in the Appropriate Place to Cause a Young Ephebe to Die and Be Resuscitated..."

Connotations Press: "At the Temple of the Ocean," "Night the City Rearranges Its Buildings to Speak to You," "Chrysalis," "Debirdcage," "Through Winter"

DIAGRAM: "Hinged," "Love Is a Burning Building"

Dogs Singing: A Tribute Anthology: "Dog," "Dog in the World," "Man with Dog"

FutureCycle Poetry: "Presto"

Gargoyle: "Lung"

Honey Land Review: "Cowgirl Guernica"

Listenlight: "Stable-Library of the Clone Shepherd"

Medulla Review: "Not Persephone"

Milk Sugar: "The Spirit in Flight"

Monkeybicycle: "Indefinite Divisibility"

No Tell Motel: "Pacific Horizon," "Waltz on Black Velvet," "Your Robot Girl"

Praxilla: "Aimless Day," "Chambers of In and Out," "Cypress"

Prime Mincer: "The Rites of Autumn," "Sleep with Accordions and Divers"

Prime Number: "Otherology"

Sakura Review: "I Give You Fresno"

Tiferet: "Dust and Stars," "Oracle," "The Garden of Hours"

Turntable & Blue Light: "Icarus in Twilight," "Flagmen in Autumn," "Garden of Earthly Delights," "Seasonal Change," and "Songbird"

The author wishes to thank his wife, C. J. Sage, for her patience and encouragement during the year when the birthday poems (over 1400 of them) were written. The author also wishes to thank Diane Kistner and Robert S. King and all of FutureCycle Press for their faith in his work and their sacrifices and dedication to publishing poetry. The author must also take a moment to acknowledge that these poems were inspired not only by the people they are directly dedicated to, but to the fans of this series who read it each day as it was unfolding, and to the terrific and numerous art pieces, movies, literature and popular song that also helped to inspire the creation of these poems.

About FutureCycle Press

FutureCycle Press is dedicated to publishing lasting English-language poetry books, chapbooks, and anthologies in both print-on-demand and ebook formats. Founded in 2007 by long-time independent editor/publishers and partners Diane Kistner and Robert S. King, the press incorporated as a nonprofit in 2012. A number of our editors are distinguished poets and writers in their own right, and we have been actively involved in the small press movement going back to the early seventies.

The FutureCycle Poetry Book Prize and honorarium is awarded annually for the best full-length volume of poetry we publish in a calendar year. Introduced in 2013, our Good Works projects are devoted to issues of universal significance, with all proceeds donated to a related worthy cause. Our Selected Poems series highlights contemporary poets with a substantial body of work to their credit.

We are dedicated to giving all of the authors we publish the care their work deserves, making our catalog of titles the most diverse and distinguished it can be, and paying forward any earnings to fund more great books.

We've learned a few things about independent publishing over the years. We've also evolved a unique, resilient publishing model that allows us to focus mainly on vetting and preserving for posterity the most books of exceptional quality without becoming overwhelmed with bookkeeping and mailing, fundraising activities, or taxing editorial and production "bubbles." To find out more about what we are doing, come see us at www.futurecycle.org.

www.ingramcontent.com/pod-product-compliance
Lightning Source LLC
Chambersburg PA
CBHW070010100426
42741CB00012B/3177